'It is not etiquette to ask a lady to take wine while eating fish or soup.'

ETIQUETTE
FOR
WINE LOVERS

Copper Beech Publishing

Published in Great Britain by
Copper Beech Publishing Ltd
© Copper Beech Publishing 2001

ISBN 1-898617-26-0
A CIP catalogue record for this book is available from
The British Library

Copper Beech Publishing Ltd
P O Box 159 East Grinstead
Sussex England RH19 4FS

WINE LOVERS

A true wine lover never permits himself to think that he is possessed of unlimited knowledge in matters relating to wines.

The wine producing districts, the intricacies of production, the history of vintages, the art of purchasing, the care with which wines should be stored and the ultimate joy of tasting the matured product, represent an intensely interesting study which occupies the whole of a lifetime!

Wine is a subject that is for ever introducing new aspects of study owing to the fact that each year produces something different to the previous vintage.

This is written with the object of placing before lovers of good wines, certain details in connection with tasting that may have escaped their attention.

WINE LOVERS

Great pleasure will be experienced by tasting wines in the orthodox fashion; and for the connoisseur, some definite rules printed as reference may be gratefully accepted with a view to guiding a young friend into the proper path of wine appreciation.

For the novice to become an expert taster or true connoisseur without years of experience is impossible. However, by following carefully the technique whereby the full quality and beauty of wine can be enjoyed, new pleasures may be found and a personal standard of wine value can be attained which will enable a person to think and talk on the subject with confidence.

SUITABLE GLASSES

... a careful study of the wine's bouquet ...

It is essential that suitable glasses are available for tasting as an 'unsuitable' glass will mar the finest of wines.

The ideal tasting glass is extremely thin.

In the event of a red wine being slightly too cold, the hands may effectively warm the wine through thin glass without delay or damage.

The glass should also be of a bulging shape and fairly narrow at the top, thereby preventing the escape of the ethers and permitting a more careful study of the wine's 'bouquet' which is, without doubt, one of its most delicate charms.

POURING AND TASTING

... rotate the glass ...

When pouring out wine with a view to tasting, the glass should not be more than half filled and it should be borne in mind that the glass should always be held as near the base as possible, particularly in the case of white wines.

After observing the colour and admiring the brilliancy of the wine, the bouquet is the next consideration for the discerning wine lover.

By carefully exercising the sense of smell a great proportion of the necessary ability to judge wine can be developed. Furthermore, it is possible to derive a considerable amount of pleasure from the art of appreciating the delicate aromas of various wines.

In order to obtain the full volume of the ethers from a wine, rotate the glass, slowly at first, then quickening the movement so as to aid the vaporisation of the perfumes. A few seconds spent in this manner ensures the release of the full aroma.

Having admired the colour of a wine and approved of its bouquet, one is then ready to taste.

By raising the glass slowly to the lips, it is possible to enjoy the aroma even more, as the smell and taste will momentarily be combined.

If, when 'nosing' a wine, the slightest suspicion of 'wood' or 'cork' can be observed, the bottle should be recorked and returned as soon as possible to the supplier, as an unclean wine should never be consumed. Any reputable wine merchant will willingly effect an exchange if a complaint is genuine.

TRAINING THE PALATE

... perfect wine has perfect harmony ...

The first mouthful of wine should not be too big; in fact it should be just sufficient to roll easily and comfortably around the mouth as this accustoms the tasting pores to the whole volume of mingling and succeeding aromas which form the cumulative flavour of the wine.

To appreciate the perfection of a fine wine the first mouthful should *not be swallowed* but discarded and a few moments may then be profitably spent in reverie; committing to memory the flavour and aroma, the beauty and characteristics that have been your good fortune to enjoy.

When training the palate, seek to memorise the characteristics of each wine that is tasted and compare with other wines of the same vintage, also with similar wines of other vintages.

It is not possible here to describe the characteristics of various wines and vintages, but in all wines, irrespective of their vintage or their country of origin, it must always be borne in mind that perfect wine has perfect harmony.

From the moment the colour is admired until the time the after-taste is enjoyed, the effect of the wine should blend into one perfect whole and when this is apparent the wine deserves every recommendation.

The corkscrew should be inserted steadily through the centre and then the cork removed without any haste or hesitation.

DECANTING

... utmost care is necessary ...

When decanting never hurry, use a slow steady movement. First remove the bottle very carefully from the bin, and place gently into a cradle. The metal capsule or wax should then be removed from the outside of the cork and the top of the bottle wiped most carefully with a clean cloth.

Red wines can throw a deposit after a certain time, therefore, it is always advisable to decant before use. The deposit thrown may vary from a light easily moveable sediment to a firm heavy crust and the utmost care is necessary when decanting because sediment will always move and can impart an undesirable flavour to the wine.

White wines should in no circumstances be decanted. In the event of there being a slight deposit, the bottle should be stood in an upright position for an hour or so before serving.

STORAGE OF WINES

... a little attention at the crucial moment ...

The precautions which have to be taken in the storage and service of wines are so simple that it is surprising that wines should so often be consumed out of condition.

Years of care are bestowed on the production and maturing of a wine. In the cultivation of the wine, right up to the time the old-bottled vintage reaches the cellar of the consumer, each and every operation has been carried out with meticulous and anxious solicitude, and any wine lover should reflect that all this could be gone for nothing for want of a little attention at the crucial moment.

The cellar:

The observance of the following simple details may be of assistance to those who take a pride in the contents of their cellar. Unpack and place into the cellar all wines as soon after delivery as possible.

If transit of red wines (especially Port) has taken place in cold weather, the wine may possibly have become chilled and will not be perfectly bright. In this case, leave for a few days in a temperature of about 65 degrees when it should regain its brilliancy.

All wines should be kept lying on their side, Port with chalk mark or label uppermost. Spirits and liqueurs should be kept standing.

White wines – still and sparkling – should be stored at a temperature of 50 degrees to 52 degrees and red wines at 58 degrees.

A good plan is to keep the cellar at an even temperature of about 55 degrees, storing white wines in the lower bin and red wines above – Port highest of all.

A GENERAL GUIDE TO
COMBINING FOOD AND WINE

Advice on the combination of food and wine is extremely difficult due to varying tastes, but the following will act as a general guide:-

APERITIF
Dry Sherry or Cocktail

HORS d'OEUVRES
Dry Sherry or Chablis

OYSTERS
Chablis or Champagne

SOUP
Medium Dry Sherry, Madeira or Marsala

FISH
Hock, Moselle, Chablis,
White Bordeaux or Champagne

A GENERAL GUIDE TO
COMBINING FOOD AND WINE

BEEF or LAMB
Burgundy or Claret

VEAL or PORK
Champagne or Sparkling Moselle

POULTRY
Champagne, Sauterne, Chablis or Graves

GAME
Burgundy, Claret or Sauterne

SWEETS
Rum, Liqueurs or Sweet Sauterne

FRUIT
Vintage or Tawny Port, Sweet Madeira

COFFEE
Old Liqueur, Brandy, Benedictine, Grand Marnier

'... *i'faith ... you have drunk too much canaries,*
and that's a marvellous searching wine, and it
perfumes the blood ere we can say "What's this?"'
Henry IV Pt 2, II.iv.;
Mistress Quickly, addressing Doll Tearsheet.

SHERRY

... supply could not meet demand ...

Sherry was Shakespeare's wine! Again and again he lauds Sherris-sack, and although the characters he used to applaud this excellent wine certainly never tasted it, Shakespeare himself loved it, lent his genius to advertising its merits, and no doubt did much towards promoting its popularity!

The wines from Xeres, near Cadiz, were natural wines, but much drier than the sweet or sweetened wine which had previously been imported from the Continent. They were sold in England as 'seck' from the Spanish 'secco' meaning dry. Later the word became further corrupted to Sack.

So popular was this Spanish wine that the supply could not meet the demand, and imitations began to flood the market from Madeira and the Canary Isles. It therefore became necessary to distinguish that which came from Xeres, and it was first called Xeres Sack, then Sherries, and finally Sherry.

Ben Jonson preferred Canary Sack, but most of his contemporaries and many poets and dramatists since have given their unreserved preference to Sherry.

When Drake raided Cadiz in 1587, he brought home 2,900 pipes of Sherry, to the great satisfaction of Elizabeth and the English – Sherry being the prime favourite of those people.

Later, in the Victorian age of prosperous, comfortable, middle-class respectability, every mahogany sideboard was graced by a decanter of Sherry. Sherry was a tradition – a token of hospitality, kindliness, comfort and steady good sense.

Sherry had been good enough for the prosperous middle-classes for generations.

This was an age of reverence – what was good enough for father, the son was proud to say, was good enough for him.

There are many varieties of Sherry, just as there are many varieties of Claret, Burgundy and Port. Those who are not very experienced in the choice of wines would do well to allow a reliable wine merchant to meet their wishes with the correct selection. Otherwise disappointment is possible, which is regrettable, especially as it is avoidable.

An inexperienced buyer might easily select a wine not at all to his taste.

Afternoon Whist Parties
*Sherry and claret cup can be provided in addition to
tea and coffee at this form of gathering, an
entertainment common in winter time.*

PORT

... the stronger head and constitution ...

Politicians Pitt the Austere and Fox the Libertine had one point in common; they both loved Port Wine.

It is said that Port Wine saved Pitt's life; it also enabled him to live; he drank gallons of it. An ailing child and a weakly youth, he became Prime Minister of England at 21 years of age, thanks to Port Wine. Pitt, steeped in Port, controlled the fortunes of England and took part in the affairs of Europe.

Fox, his brilliant opponent, swilled Port like a brute, and recuperated like a genius in order to attack with a clear and sober brain the man whose equally clever brain was fed on and sustained by Port.

At that time it was fashion to drink this wine from Portugal.

Those who could drink the most, were thought to be possessed of the strongest brains.

Port is a heavy wine, thus the more a man drank the stronger head and constitution he was supposed to have and, those who had not the necessary strength adopted an air of bravado and often drank more than those who could do so with impunity.

Those were reckless days in the time of a reckless Regent, but the wine was good and men were hard, and the more Port Wine they drank the more revenue it brought to the State and the firmer was our relation with Portugal. At this time men were taught to 'Love Duty, Honour the King and Hate a Frenchman like the Devil'.

The grapes are found at their best in the mountainous region of the Upper Douro, Portugal.

To the naturally fermented product is added brandy. This has the effect of giving body to the wine. It checks fermentation and allows the wine to retain some of the natural sweetness of the grape.

The wine, made in the vineyards on the beautiful slopes of the Douro, is then floated down the river in barges to Oporto, where it is stored in lodges to mature.

This takes at least ten years of constant care, during which time it is frequently tested by men who have served a lifetime in gaining the necessary experience to know exactly when the wine is ready for bottling and how long it should remain in bottle when offering it for sale, and what price it will fetch.

*At dessert, Port, Sherry, Claret and Madeira
are placed on the table.*

*A good Burgundy ...
on the whole the wine most suited
for consumption during the chilly and damp
autumn and winter days.*

BURGUNDY

… the finest restorative …

The mellow and fruity flavour of a good Burgundy renders it on the whole the wine most suited for consumption during the chilly and damp autumn and winter days in this country.

It is a fallacy to imagine that Burgundy must inevitably be a heavy wine. Caressingly soft and silky, yes; but some of the finest growths possess less body than many a Claret.

Burgundy stimulates natural warmth and vigour, tones up the nervous system, strengthens the heart and fortifies the brain.

It is one of the finest restoratives after illness, overwork, or overstrain. Burgundy is also a recognised preventive of illness during a run-down condition. Consult a good wine merchant to rely on his experience and knowledge.

'One of the great charms of Claret is that it adapts itself to all tastes, constitutions and purses.'

'The varieties of Claret, the differences in excellence and in price, in type and style, are much greater than is the case with any other wine.'

The above two quotations are from 'Wines and Spirits' by A.L. Simon.

CLARET

... a delicious smoothness ...

In Claret there is a more perfect harmony between its component parts than in any other wine. There is neither a lack nor an excess of grape-sugar, acidity, tannin or alcohol, all of which so marvellously harmonise that Claret charms without ever palling on the palate and stimulates the brain without ever over-balancing it.

It is indeed the very multiplicity of choice which renders it difficult sometimes to fit the exact wine to the individual palate.

In the Medoc alone there are some sixty communes and villages, each possessing a variety of growths with their own characteristics, but nevertheless a family likeness. The St Emilion and allied districts differ from Medoc in character, being softer and fruitier with possible less finesse. The numerous red Graves are famous for a delicious smoothness.

Claret contains a quantity of iron
and is a cure for anaemia –
a malady which is practically unknown
in the Bordeaux district.

CLARET AS A CURE FOR INDIGESTION

... those who suffer in this way ...

Claret is also a very excellent and exceedingly pleasant specific for dyspepsia and all milder forms of indigestion and troubles arising therefrom.

To indigestion can also be traced headaches, lassitude, disinclination to work, introspection and melancholia. Those who suffer in this way might try the effect of a course of Claret!

The cure is cheap by comparison with the general suffering. The medical profession knows an enormous number of people with this complaint, yet the wine merchant could cure the majority!

To indigestion can be traced chronic bad temper, irritability, grumbling and sourness of disposition.

HOCK & MOSELLE

... for those suffering from gout ...

Progressive **increase** in the consumption of Hocks and Moselles during the past few years occasions no surprise.

Just as Claret and Burgundy satisfy the desire for red wines, white wines - the Hocks and Moselles - are most pleasing to the average palate.

When dry, they are seldom insipid and even the richest varieties never cloy and can therefore be taken with enjoyment throughout a meal.

Moselle achieved great popularity during the Edwardian era as the favourite beverage of King Edward VII.

These wines are particularly recommended for their dietetic advantages for those suffering from gout, rheumatism or allied ailments or tendencies.

*It is not etiquette to ask a lady to take wine
while eating fish or soup.
Soup and wine, or fish and wine, do not agree.
If you ask a lady she cannot well refuse
and by obliging you, she will destroy
the flavour of the fish or soup
to her own palate.*

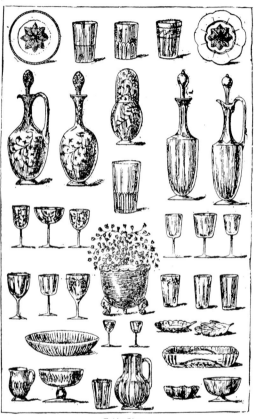

Table Glass.

CHOICE OF GLASS

... those who like dainty articles ...

Not a little of the handsome appearance of a well-set dinner-table may be ascribed to its array of shining well-polished glass.

The table glass should be of as good quality as possible, and the design should be characterised by its refined simplicity.

Too much design and ornamentation is a mistake! It robs glass of that bright transparency which forms the great charm of its appearance. But unless the glass is always under the care of a reliable servant, buy some of not too fine a quality and of a design that can be easily replaced. Very thin glass is no doubt appreciated by those who like dainty articles, but it requires the utmost care in the washing and drying. When cut glass cannot be afforded, plain glass with a little engraving looks the best.

CARE OF THE WINE GLASS

... if a little vinegar is added ...

Glass requires very special care if it is to look nice. Glasses should be washed first in warm water, with a very little soap or a few drops of ammonia, using the fingers or a fine cloth to rub them with. Then rinse them in clear cold water and place them upside down on a tray to drain.

The greatest care must be taken in the drying, because of the slender stems. If a little vinegar is added occasionally to the water in which table glass is rinsed, it will give it an extra brightness. Care must be taken, too, that the towel is dry and free from grease, or it would give the glass a smeared appearance.

When a glass has been used for milk or any other liquid of a greasy nature, it should be filled with cold water as soon as possible to prevent the grease sinking into the glass and making it troublesome to wash.

The greatest care must be taken in the drying,
because of the slender stems.

Sometimes a brush is an assistance in the washing of decanters.

CARE OF DECANTERS

... one part coarse salt to two parts vinegar ...

When these become stained or discoloured, they may be treated in one of the following ways:

Fill the bottle half-full of warm soapy water, and put in some pieces of brown paper, some tea-leaves or small pieces of raw potato; shake occasionally, then pour out, rinse and drain. Crushed egg shells or fine ashes used with a little soap can also be good. If none of these removes the stain, try one part coarse salt to two parts vinegar, undiluted with water.

If the stoppers become fixed in decanters, it is a good plan to pour a few drops of oil round the neck and place the decanter near the fire. If it still sticks, wash it in warm water and repeat. Sometimes a few gentle taps with another stopper will help to loosen the fixed one. Glycerine can be used instead of oil.

**Decanters should never be put away
with the dregs in them.**

DEFECTIVE WINES

A good butler will find out when decanting ...

However well decanted, a defective wine, or wine which smells of the cork, must not be served.

You come across bottles that are not perfect, which is mainly due to carelessness in bottling. Such wine the good butler will find out when decanting, generally by the bouquet or want of bouquet, or eventually by fungus or corky smell. Any such defective bottle should be discarded, and if not too bad, poured into the receptacle destined for kitchen use.

HOW TO SERVE

Serving:

White wines should be served cold; they may be iced, but ice should never be put in the wine. Where a refrigerator is available, place the bottle in it with cork undrawn about an hour before serving.

Red wines should be served at the temperature of the dining-room. They should be brought slowly to this temperature, the cork being drawn first.

Never warm a red wine quickly, either by dipping the bottle or decanter in hot water or placing the wine near a fire.

Decant old Claret an hour before dinner and old Port an hour earlier. By placing the decanted wine in the dining room with the stopper out of the decanter the wine may 'breathe' and acquire the temperature of the room gradually and harmlessly and be at its best when placed on the table. Never serve fine wines or fine Brandy in small glasses. Use large glasses that are only half filled as the bouquet can never be appreciated if the glass is too small or too full.

It is essential that both decanters and glasses are kept faultlessly clean and it is advisable to keep cloths exclusively for this purpose as the finest wine is ruined if served in glasses that have been polished with an unclean cloth.

DINNER IN HOUSES WHERE A BUTLER IS EMPLOYED

The following indications, namely, the when and what to serve at a special time, will forever be subjects for controversy amongst diners-out, gourmets and all lovers of good living. These in general lines are an indication for the now customary dinner in houses where butlers are employed.

Hors d'oeuvres

The serving of hors d'oeuvres at the commencement of luncheon or dinner has been introduced in imitation of our Scandinavian and Russian neighbours, who wash down their sardines, caviar, anchovies, or other appetizing delicacies with Schnapps of all kinds! This may do for Russian or Swedish society, but I am glad to say this nasty habit of taking spirits before dinner has not yet been introduced here!

***Indeed, it is unlikely that anyone wants to drink
with our nice little hors d'oeuvres; but if a drink is
wanted, nothing will do so well as
a small glass of dry sherry.***

Oysters

Next we come to oysters, which should be accompanied with the lightest Moselle, Hock or Chablis. Light because the oyster, being very delicate, suggests that the accompanying wine should be delicate, too, and so as not in any way to cloy the palate. Therefore a sweetish white wine such as Sauterne, or, indeed, any sparkling wine, is out of place.

Do not repeat; one glass is enough unless you are asked for more wine, more particularly as the soup should be served immediately on removal of the oyster plate.

Hot soup

Be sure that the soup has been taken before you serve any further wine; there should be no hurry. Whilst the soup plates are being removed, a small glass of sherry or madeira may be poured out; it should always be fine wine – in fact, the finest you can afford.

After hot soup has been taken, the palate is most keen, and any slight defect or common flavour comes out; therefore you must serve the best you can.

The butler should induce the cook not to pepper the soup – it spoils the taste of the wine after!

Fish

With fish, if white and served with plain sauce, the wine that goes best is Hock or Chablis, whilst with heavier fish such as salmon, you should give the preference to Sauterne or Hock of very fine and fruit quality. Champagne after fish is simply bad, and red wines are lost.

The drinking of dry champagne with all kinds of food is not commendable. Gastronomically it is wrong, because champagne does not go with everything.

Entrees

With your entrees you should commence to serve claret, and to those who prefer it continue the white wines that were served with the fish. Dry champagne should only be offered with the roast, and burgundy with the game, but there will be room for the high-class claret from the entrees onward until the sweets make their appearance.

It is hoped that wine in plenty and of good quality is served in even more frugal households. Red wine, such as claret, being more invigorating through being more tonic, is generally preferable to white, where one and the same wine is served at the meal.

Desserts and cheese

You should stop serving any more as soon as sweets are being taken, likewise with the cheese; then port, sherry or madeira are the only suitable wines, and those dessert wines are the only ones fit for after-dinner or luncheon purposes.

Some years ago fine clarets were served as dessert wines; this is a great error. A fine claret, however superb in quality, tastes tart after pudding and sweets or fruit; its proper place is with the roast or game, or even with entrees.

The waiter holds a clean napkin round the neck of the bottle. In hot weather, ice is handed round in a glass dish with ice tongs.

The host fills the glass of the lady on his right, if she wishes it, and the decanters make the tour of the table, returning to the host, with whom they remain till the ladies have left the room.

MULLED WINE

Mulled wine can be warming and a perfect welcome to guests on a winter's evening.

Ingredients

To every pint of wine allow one large cupful of water, sugar and spice to taste.

In making preparations it is very difficult to give the exact proportions of ingredients like sugar and spice, as what quantity might suit one person would be to another quite distasteful.

Boil the spices in the water until the flavour is extracted, then add the wine and sugar, and bring the whole to the boiling point, when ready serve with strips of crisp dry toast, or with biscuits.

The spices usually used for mulled wine are cloves, grated nutmeg and cinnamon or mace.

Any kind of wine may be mulled, but port and claret are those usually selected for the purpose.

MULLED WINE

The vessel

The vessel that the wine is boiled in must be delicately clean, and should be kept exclusively for the purpose. Small tin warmers or mulls may be purchased for a trifle, which are more suitable than saucepans, as, if the latter are not scrupulously clean, they will spoil the wine, by imparting to it a very disagreeable flavour.

These warmers should be used for no other purpose.

MULL.

A FEW RULES ...

A few rules which should be observed when dealing with one of nature's most delightful and certainly most harmonious products, are as follows: –

1. It is always inadvisable to smoke just before tasting because by tainting the palate the wine that follows is naturally tainted.

2. The finest way to clean the palate is to eat a small piece of crusty bread or a dry biscuit.

3. It is well worth while to train a butler to appreciate good wine as you may rest assured that when he understands and knows wines, he will look after them with reverence and decant them with care.

A GUIDE FOR THE BUTLER

In his cellar a good butler will need:

Good corkscrews
Knife
Ullage bottle
One small funnel
Corks
Candlestick
Matchbox

A good butler will know that the condition of his glass and decanter is as necessary for fine wines as the brightness of his boots is for the morning appearance of a gentleman!

Sherry before dinner has a tonic effect. It is the perfect appetiser and also the only wine that can be appreciated whilst smoking. Sherry contains more iron than any other wine, and is a splendid tonic and blood-maker. It is the only wine in the Pharmacopoeia mentioned for the preparation of medical wines.

These words for wine lovers have been collected from books of etiquette and the booklets of wine merchants from days gone by.

Every effort has been made to trace ownership of these quotations. If any omission has occurred it is inadvertent and it should be brought to the attention of the publisher.

THE ETIQUETTE COLLECTION *Collect the set!*

ETIQUETTE FOR COFFEE LOVERS
Fresh coffee - the best welcome in the world!
Enjoy the story of coffee drinking,
coffee etiquette and recipes.

ETIQUETTE FOR CHOCOLATE LOVERS
Temptation through the years.
A special treat for all Chocolate Lovers.

THE ETIQUETTE OF NAMING THE BABY
'A good name keeps its lustre in the dark.'
Old English Proverb

THE ETIQUETTE OF AN ENGLISH TEA
How to serve a perfect English afternoon tea;
traditions, superstitions, recipes and how to read your
fortune in the tea-leaves afterwards.

THE ETIQUETTE OF ENGLISH PUDDINGS
Traditional recipes for good old-fashioned
puddings - together with etiquette notes
for serving.

ETIQUETTE FOR GENTLEMEN
*'If you have occasion to use your handkerchief
do so as noiselessly as possible.'*

A Copper Beech Book makes the perfect gift.

ETIQUETTE FOR THE TRAVELLER
'There is nothing that a man can less afford to leave at home than his conscience or his good habits.'

ETIQUETTE FOR THE WELL-DRESSED MAN
A man is judged by his appearance.
'If you wear a morning coat your trousers will show more and must therefore be absolutely blameless.'

THE ETIQUETTE OF MOTORING
'Never take a sharp corner at full speed. A walking pace would be much better.'

THE ETIQUETTE OF DRESS
Learn how to be correctly dressed for all occasions.
A fine gift for anyone with an interest in fashion.

For your free catalogue, write to:

Copper Beech Publishing Ltd
P O Box 159 East Grinstead Sussex England RH19 4FS
www.copperbeechpublishing.co.uk

Copper Beech Gift Books
are designed and printed
in Great Britain